I0468375

The GOAL

Diggerz

A Guide To Unlocking Your Full Potential And Achieving Success

Leslie J. Garcia

The GOAL Diggerz

Copyright © 2016

All rights reserved. No part of this book may be reproduced, stored in a retrieval system, or transmitted in any form or by any means, electronic, mechanical, photocopying, recording, scanning, or otherwise, without the prior written permission of the publisher.

The GOAL Diggerz

TABLE OF CONTENTS

Introduction

There has never been more opportunities for creative and determined people to achieve more of their goals than they can today. Regardless of short-term ups and downs in the economy and in your life, we are entering into an age of peace and prosperity superior to any previous era in human history.

When I first became a single mother, I was filled with so much shame and guilt, I felt like such a failure to myself and to my family. I was lost. I saw myself as forever relying on food stamps and public housing. That was the last thing I wanted to be, for my children especially.

Now looking at my own personal journey, I have always worked the entire time and I have been on my own with my 2 children. I first started off in retail then moved my way up to customer service, then admin assistant to a major financial firm, buyer to large pharma companies, and most recently, a Business Analyst to various corporations.

Although I was now making a decent salary, I still felt unhappy. I would drag myself into work every morning hating every single minute of it. I could not even concentrate for long periods of time on my projects at work because all I could ever think about was how unhappy I was. I always felt like I could be doing so much more than just sitting in some stuffy office building, building someone else's dream. I wanted to build my own. I wanted to feel the sun on my face. But all I could do was drag through my days only to leave work run down and wanting nothing more than my bed. The next day I would wake up and do it all over again. I thought this was the path to being a Successful Single Mother....how wrong I was.

I decided that I wasn't letting yet another year go by confused and waiting for my dream life to plop into my lap. It was time to do something completely different. I took massive risks, got seriously productive, invested in support and launched my brand.

I am on a personal mission to change the way we view ourselves as women, not just by talking about it but by making sure to reach out to other women. Here's to all the fabulous successful women out there – keep going, you're doing an awesome job!

In the pages ahead, you will learn the most important ideas and strategies ever discovered for achieving everything that you could ever want in life as a woman. You will find that there are no limits to what you can accomplish except for the limits you place on your own imagination. And since there are no limits to what you can imagine, there are no limits to what you can achieve. This is one of the greatest discoveries of all. Let us begin.

"The greatest discovery of all time is that a person can change his future by merely changing his attitude." - Oprah Winfrey

CHAPTER 1
Unlock Your Potential

The potential of the average person is like a huge ocean unsailed, a new continent unexplored, a world of possibilities waiting to be released and channeled toward some great good.

Success is goals, and all else is commentary. All successful people are intensely goal oriented. They know what they want and they are focused single mindedly on achieving it, every single day.

Your ability to set goals is the master skill of success. Goals unlock your positive mind and release ideas and energy for goal attainment. Without goals, you simply drift and flow on the currents of life. With goals, you fly like an arrow, straight and true to your target.

The truth is that you probably have more natural potential than you could use if you lived one hundred lifetimes. Whatever you have accomplished up until now is only a small fraction of what is truly possible for you. One of the rules for success is this, it doesn't matter where you're coming from; all that matters is where you're going.

And where you are going is solely determined by yourself and your own thoughts.

Clear goals increase your confidence, develop your competence and boost your levels of motivation. As sales trainer Tom Hopkins says, Goals are the fuel in the furnace of achievement.

You Create Your Own World

Perhaps the greatest discovery in human history is the power of your mind to create the aspects of your life. Everything you see around you in the man-made world began as a thought or an idea in the mind of a single person before it was translated into reality.

Everything in your life started as a thought, a wish, a hope or a dream, either in your mind, or in the mind of someone else. Your thoughts are creative. Your thoughts form and shape your world and everything that happens to you.

The great summary statement of all religions, philosophies, metaphysics, psychology and success is this: "You become what you think about — most of the time." Your outer world ultimately becomes a reflection of your inner world, and mirrors back to you what you think about. Whatever you think about continuously emerges in your reality.

Many thousands of successful people have been asked what it is that they think about most of the time. The most common answer given by successful people is that they think about what they want, and how to get it most of the time.

Unsuccessful, unhappy people think and talk about what they don't want most of the time. They talk about their problems and worries, and who is to blame, most of the time. But successful people keep their thoughts and conversation on the topics of their most intensely desired goals. They think and talk about what they want most of the time.

Living without clear goals is like driving in a thick fog. No matter how powerful or well-engineered your car, you drive slowly, hesitantly, making little progress on even the smoothest road.

Deciding upon your goals clears the fog immediately and allows you to focus and channel your energies and abilities. Clear goals enable you to step on the accelerator of your own life and leap ahead rapidly toward achieving more of the things you really want.

Your Automatic Goal Seeking Function

Imagine this exercise: you take a homing pigeon out of its roost, put it in a cage, cover the cage with a blanket, put the cage in a box and then place the box into a closed truck cab. You can then drive a thousand miles in any direction. If you then open the truck cab, take out the box, take off the blanket and let the homing pigeon out of the cage, the homing pigeon will fly up into the air, circle three times and then fly unerringly back to its home roost a thousand miles away.

This is the only creature on earth that has this incredible cybernetic, goal-seeking function, except for man.

You have the same goal achieving ability as the homing pigeon, but with one marvelous addition. When you are absolutely clear about your goal, you do not even have to know where it is or how it is to be achieved. By simply deciding exactly what it is you want, you will begin to move unerringly toward your goal, and your goal will start to move unerringly toward you. At exactly the right time, and in exactly the right place, you and the goal will meet.

Because of this incredible cybernetic mechanism located deep within your mind, you always achieve your goals, whatever they are. You move toward them and they move toward you. If your goal is to get home at night and watch television, you will almost certainly achieve it. If your goal is to create a wonderful life full of health, happiness and prosperity, you will achieve that as well. Like a computer, your goal seeking mechanism is non-judgmental. It works automatically and continuously to bring you what you want, regardless of what you program into it.

Nature doesn't care about the size or scope of your goals. If you set little goals, your automatic goal achieving mechanism will enable you to achieve little goals. If you set large goals, this natural capability will enable you to achieve large goals. The size, scope and detail of the goals you choose to think about most of the time is completely up to you.

Why People Don't Set Goals

Here is a good question: If goal setting is automatic, why is it that so few people have clear, written, measurable, time-bounded goals that they work toward each day? This is one of the great mysteries of life. I believe there are four reasons why people don't set goals.

1. Goals Aren't Important

First, most people don't realize the importance of goals. If you grow up in a home where no one has goals, or you socialize with a group where goals are neither discussed nor valued, you can very easily reach adulthood without knowing that your ability to set and achieve goals will have more of an effect on your life than any other skill.

Look around you. How many of your friends or family members are clear and committed to their goals?

2. They Don't Know How

The second reason that people don't have goals is because they don't know how to set them in the first place. Even worse, many people think that they already have goals, when in reality, what they actually have are a series of wishes or dreams like, "Be happy," or "Make a lot of money," or "Have a nice family life."

But these are not goals at all. They are merely fantasies that are common to everyone. A goal however is something distinctly different from a wish. It is clear, written and specific. It can be quickly and easily described to another person. You can measure it, and you know when you have achieved it, or not.

It is possible to take an advanced degree at a leading university without ever receiving one hour of instruction on goal setting. It is almost as if the people who determine the educational content of our schools and universities are completely blind to the importance of goal setting in achieving success later in life. And of course, if you never hear about goals until you are an adult, as I experienced, you will have no idea how important they are to everything you do.

3. The Fear of Failure

The third reason that people don't set goals is because of the fear of failure.

Failure hurts. It is emotionally and often financially painful and distressing. Everyone has had failure experiences from time to time. Each time, they resolve to be more careful next time and avoid failure experiences in the future. They then make the mistake of unconsciously sabotaging themselves by not setting any goals at which they might fail. They end up going through life functioning at far lower levels than are truly possible for them.

4. The Fear of Rejection

The fourth reason that people don't set goals is because of the fear of rejection. People are afraid that if they set a goal and are not successful, others will criticize or ridicule them. This is one of the reasons why, when you begin to set goals, you should keep your goals confidential. Don't tell anyone. Let them see by your results and achievements what you have accomplished, but don't tell them in advance. What they don't know can't hurt you.

Join The Top Three Percent

Mark McCormack in his book "What They Don't Teach You In The Harvard Business School" tells of a Harvard study conducted between 1979 and 1989. In 1979, the graduates of the MBA program at Harvard were asked, "Have you set clear, written goals for your future and made plans to accomplish them?" It turned out that only 3% of the graduates had written goals and plans. 13% had goals, but they were not in writing. Fully 84% had no specific goals at all, aside from getting out of school and enjoying the summer.

Ten years later, in 1989, they interviewed the members of that class again. They found that the 13% who had goals, but which were not in writing were earning on average twice as much as the 84% of students who had no goals at all. But most surprisingly, they found that the 3% of graduates who had clear, written goals when they left Harvard were earning, on average, ten times as much as the other 97% of graduates all together. The only difference between the groups was the clarity of the goals they had for themselves when they started out.

No Road Signs

The importance of clarity is easy to understand. Imagine arriving on the outskirts of a large city and being told to drive to a particular home or office in that city. But here's the catch. There are no road signs and you have no map of the city. In fact, all you are given is a very general description of the home or office that is your goal. Here is the question: How long do you think it would take you to find a home or office in a city without a road map or without road signs?

The answer is: Probably your whole life. If you ever did find the home or office, it would be very much a matter of luck. And sadly enough, this is the way most people live their lives.

The average person starts life traveling through an unmapped and uncharted world with no road map. This is the equivalent of starting off in life with no goals and plans. He or she simply figures things out as he or she goes along. Often, ten or twenty years of work will go past and the individual is still broke, unhappy in his or her job, dissatisfied with his or her marriage and making little progress. And still, he or she goes home every night and watches television, wishing and hoping that things would get better. But they seldom do. Not by themselves.

Happiness Requires Goals

Earl Nightingale once wrote: Happiness is the progressive realization of a worthy ideal, or goal.

You only feel truly happy when you are making progress, step-by- step, toward something that is important to you. Victor Frankl, the founder of

Logotherapy, wrote that the greatest need of the human being is for a sense of meaning and purpose in life.

Goals give you a sense of meaning and purpose. Goals give you a sense of direction. As you move toward your goals you feel happier and stronger. You feel more energized and effective. You feel more confident and competent in yourself and your abilities. Every step you take toward your goals increases your belief that you can set and achieve even bigger goals in the future.

More people today fear change, and worry about the future, than at any other time in our history. One of the great benefits of goal setting is that goals enable you to control the direction of change in your life.

Goals enable you to assure that the changes in your life are largely self-determined and self-directed. Goals enable you to instill meaning and purpose into everything you do.

One of the most important teachings of Aristotle, the Greek philosopher, was that man is a teleological organism. The word "teleos" in Greek means goals. What Aristotle concluded was that all human action is purposeful in some way. You are only happy when you are doing something that is moving you toward something that you want. The great questions then become: What are your goals?

What purposes are you aiming at? Where do you want to end up at the end of the day?

Clarity Is Everything

Your inborn potential is extraordinary. You have within you, right now, the ability to achieve almost any goal that you can set for yourself. Your greatest responsibility to yourself is to invest whatever time is required to become absolutely clear about exactly what it is you want, and how you can best achieve it. The greater clarity you have regarding your true goals, the more of your potential you will unleash for good in your life.

You have probably heard it said that the average person uses only 10% of his or her potential. The sad fact is that, according to Stanford University, the average person functions with only about 2% of his or her mental potential. The remainder just sits there in reserve, being saved up for some later time. This would be exactly as if your parents had left you a trust fund with $100,000 in it, but all you ever took out to spend was $2,000. The other $98,000 dollars simply sat in the account unused throughout your life.

Develop A Burning Desire

The starting point of all goal attainment is desire. You must develop an intense, burning desire for your goals if you really want to achieve them. It is only when your desire becomes intense enough that you will have the energy and the internal drive to overcome all the obstacles that will arise in your path.

The good news is that almost anything that you want long enough and hard enough, you can ultimately achieve.

The great oil billionaire, H. L. Hunt, was once asked the "secret of success." He replied that success required two things, and two things only. First, he said, you must know exactly what it is you want. Most people never make this decision. Second, he said, you must determine the price that you will have to pay to achieve it, and then get busy paying that price.

The Cafeteria Model of Success

Life is more like a buffet or cafeteria than it is a restaurant. In a restaurant, you eat the complete dinner and then you pay the bill. But in a buffet or cafeteria, you have to serve yourself, and pay in full before you enjoy the meal. Many people make the mistake of thinking that they will pay the price after they have experienced the success. They sit in front of the stove of life and say, "First give me some heat, and then I'll put in some wood."

As motivational speaker Zig Ziglar once said, "The elevator to success is out of service. But the stairs are always open."

Another important observation from Aristotle was his conclusion that the ultimate purpose of all human action is the achievement of personal happiness. Whatever you do, he said, it is aimed at increasing your happiness in some way. You may or may not be successful in achieving happiness, but your happiness is always your ultimate aim.

The Key To Happiness

Setting goals, working toward them day-by-day, and ultimately achieving them is the key to happiness in life. Goal setting is so powerful that the very act of thinking about your goals makes you happy, even before you have taken the first step toward achieving them.

To unlock and unleash your full potential, you should make a habit of daily goal setting and achieving for the rest of your life. You should develop a laser-like focus so that you are always thinking and talking about the things you want rather than the things that you don't want. You must resolve, from this moment on, to be a goal- seeking organism, like a guided missile, or a homing pigeon, moving unerringly toward the things that are important to you.

There is no greater guarantee of a long, happy, healthy and prosperous life than for you to be continually working on being, having and achieving more and more of the things you really want. Clear goals enable you to release your full potential for personal and professional success. Goals enable you to overcome any obstacle, and to make your future unlimited.

Unlock Your Potential:

1. Imagine that you have the inborn ability to achieve any goal you could ever set for yourself. What do you really want to be, have and do?

2. What are the activities that give you your greatest sense of meaning and purpose in life?

3. Look at your personal and work life today and identify how your own thinking has created your world. What should you, could you change?

4. What do you think and talk about most of the time, what you want, or what you don't want?

5. What is the price you will have to pay to achieve the goals that are most important to you?

6. What one action should you take immediately as the result of your answers to the above questions?

CHAPTER 2
Create Your Own Future

In more than 3300 studies of leaders conducted over the years, there is a special quality that stands out, one quality that all great leaders have in common. It is the quality of vision. Leaders have vision. Non- leaders do not.

Earlier I said that the most important discovery in all of human history is that, "You become what you think about — most of the time." What is it then that leaders think about, most of the time? And the answer is that leaders think about the future and where they are going, and what they can do to get there.

Non-leaders, on the other hand, think about the present, and the pleasures and problems of the moment. They think and worry about the past, and what has happened that cannot be changed.

Think About The Future

We call this leadership quality "Future-Orientation." Leaders think about the future and what they want to accomplish, and where they want to arrive sometime down the road. Leaders think about what they want, and what can be done to achieve it. The good news is that, when you begin to think about your future as well, you begin to think like a leader, and you will soon get the same results that leaders get.

Dr. Edward Banfield of Harvard concluded, after more than 50 years of research, that "long-time perspective" was the most important determinant of financial and personal success in life. Banfield defined long-time perspective as the "ability to think several years into the future while making decisions in the present." This is one of the most important discoveries ever made. Just think! The further you think into the future, the better decisions you will make in the present to assure that that future becomes a reality.

Become A Millionaire

For example, if you save $100 per month from the age of 20 to the age of 65, and you invested that money in a mutual fund earning an average of 10% per annum over time, you would be worth more than $1,118,000 dollars when you retired.

Anyone who really wanted to could save $100 per month, if he or she had a long enough time perspective. What this means is that every single person starting work today can become a millionaire over time if they begin early enough, save consistently enough, and hold to their long-term vision of financial independence.

Create A Five Year Fantasy

In personal strategic planning, you should begin with a long-term view of your life, as well. You should begin by practicing idealization in everything you do. In the process of idealization, you create a five-year fantasy for yourself, and begin thinking about what your life would look like in five years if it were perfect in every respect.

The biggest single obstacle to setting goals is "self-limiting beliefs." These are areas where you believe yourself to be limited in some way. You may believe yourself to be inadequate or inferior in areas such as intelligence, ability, talent, creativity, personality or something else. As a result, you sell yourself short. By underestimating yourself, you set either no goals, or low goals that are far below what you are truly capable of accomplishing.

Imagine No Limitations

By combining idealization and future-orientation, you cancel or neutralize this process of self-limitation. You imagine for the moment that you have no limitations at all. You imagine that you have all the time, talents and abilities you could ever require to achieve any goal you could set for yourself. No matter where you are in life, you imagine that you have all the friends, contacts and relationships you need to open every door and achieve anything you could really want. You imagine that you have no limitations whatsoever on what you could be, have or do in the pursuit of the goals that are really important to you.

Practice Blue Sky Thinking

In Charles Garfield's studies of "Peak Performers," he made an interesting discovery. He analyzed men and women who had achieved only average results at work for many years, but who suddenly exploded into great success and accomplishment. He found that at the "take-off point," every one of them began engaging in what he called "Blue Sky Thinking."

In blue-sky thinking, you imagine that all things are possible for you, just like looking up into a clear blue sky, with no limits. You project forward several years and imagine that your life were perfect in every respect sometime in the future. You then look back to where you are today and ask yourself this question:

"What would have to have happened for me to have created my perfect future?" You then come back to where you are in the present in your own mind, and you ask, "What would have to happen from this point forward for me to achieve all my goals sometime in the future?"

Refuse To Compromise Your Dreams

When you practice idealization and future-orientation, you make no compromises with your dreams and visions for yourself and your future.

You don't settle for smaller goals or half successes. Instead, you "dream big dreams" and project forward mentally as though you are one of the most powerful people in the universe. You create your perfect future. You decide what you really want, before you come back to the present moment and deal with what is possible for you within your current situation.

Start with your business and career. Imagine that your work life was perfect five years from now. Answer these questions:

- What would it look like?

- What would you be doing?

- Where would you be doing it?

- Who would you be working with? What level of responsibility would you have?

- What kind of skills and abilities would you have?

- What kind of goals would you be accomplishing?

- What level of status would you have in your field?

Practice No Limit Thinking

When you answer these questions, imagine that you have no limits. Imagine that everything is possible for you. Peter Drucker once said, "We greatly overestimate what we can accomplish in one year. But we greatly underestimate what we can accomplish in five years." Don't let this happen to you.

Now, idealize your perfect financial life sometime in the future:

- How much do you want to be earning five years from today?

- What sort of lifestyle do you want to have? What kind of home do you want to live in?

- What kind of car do you want to drive?

- What kind of material luxuries do you want to provide for yourself and your family?

- How much do you want to have in the bank?

- How much do you want to be saving and investing each month and each year?

- How much do you want to be worth when you retire? Imagine that you have a "magic slate." You can write down anything you want. You can erase anything that may have happened in the past, and create whatever picture you desire for your future. You can clean the slate at any time and start over. You have no limits.

Imagine Your Perfect Family Life

Look at your family and relationships today, and project five years into the future:

- If your family life were perfect five years from now, what would it look like?

- Who would you be with? Who would you no longer be with?

- Where and how would you be living?

- What kind of living standards would you have?

- What kind of relationships would you have with the most important people in your life, five years from now, if everything were perfect in every respect?

When you fantasize and imagine your perfect future, the only question you ask is, "How?" This is the most powerful question of all. Asking it repeatedly stimulates your creativity and triggers ideas to help you accomplish your goals. Unsuccessful people always wonder whether or not a particular goal is possible. High achievers on the other hand only ask the question, "How?" They then set to work to find ways to make their visions and goals into realities.

Ideal Health and Fitness

Review your levels of health and fitness in every area:

- If you were a perfect physical specimen five years from now, how would you look, feel and appear?

- What would be your ideal weight?

- How much would you exercise each week?

- What would be your overall level of health?

- What changes would you have to start making today in your diet, exercise routines and health habits to enjoy superb physical health sometime in the future?

You then imagine that you are an important and influential person, a "player" in your community. You are making a significant contribution to the world around you. You are making a difference with your life and in the lives of other people. If your social and community status and involvement were ideal:

- What would you be doing?

- What organizations would you be working with or contributing to?

- What are the causes that you strongly believe in and support, and how could you become more involved in those areas?

Just Do It!

The primary difference between high achievers and low achievers is "action-orientation." Men and women who accomplish tremendous things in life are intensely action oriented. They are moving all the time. They are always busy. If they have an idea, they take action on it immediately.

On the other hand, low achievers and non-achievers are full of good intentions, but they always have an excuse for not taking action today. It is well said that, "the road to hell is paved with good intentions."

Examine yourself in terms of your personal inventory of skills, knowledge, talent, education and ability. If you were developed to the highest level possible for you (and there is virtually no limit), answer these questions:

- What additional knowledge and skills would you have acquired five years from now?

- In what areas would you be recognized as absolutely excellent in what you do?

- What would you be doing each day in order to develop the knowledge and skills you need to be one of the top performers in your field sometime in the future?

Once you have answered these questions, the only question you ask is, "How?" How do you attain the skills and expertise you will require to lead your field in the years ahead?

Design Your Perfect Calendar

Especially, decide how you would like to live, day in and day out, your ideal lifestyle. Design your perfect calendar, from January 1st to December 31st:

- What would you like to do on your weekends and vacations?

- How much time would you like to take off each week, month and year?

- Where would you like to go?

- How would you organize your year if you had no limitations, and complete control over your time?

In the Bible it says, "Where there is no vision, the people perish." What this means is that, if you lack an exciting vision for your future, you will "perish" inside in terms of lacking motivation and enthusiasm for what you are doing. But the reverse of this is that, with an exciting future vision, you will be continuously motivated and stimulated every day to take the actions necessary to make your ideal vision a reality.

The Key To Happiness

You remember that, "Happiness is the progressive realization of a worthy ideal." When you have clear, exciting goals and ideals, you will feel happier about yourself and your world. You will be more positive and optimistic. You will be more cheerful and enthusiastic. You will feel internally motivated to get up and get going every morning, because every step you are taking will be moving you in the direction of something that is important to you.

Resolve to think about your ideal future most of the time. Remember, the very best days of your life lie ahead. The happiest moments you will ever experience are still to come. The highest income you will ever earn is going to materialize in the months and years ahead. The future is going to be better than anything that may have happened in your past. There are no limits.

The clearer you can be about your long term future, the more rapidly you will attract people and circumstances into your life to help make that future a reality. The greater clarity you have about who you are and what you want, the more you will achieve and the faster you will achieve it in every area of your life.

Create Your Own Future:

• Imagine that there is a solution to every problem, a way to overcome every limitation, and no limit on your achicving every goal you can set for yourself. What would you do differently?

- Practice "back from the future thinking." Project forward five years and look back to the present. What would have to have happened for your world to be ideal?

- Imagine your financial life were perfect in every way. How much would you be earning? How much would you be worth? What steps could you take, starting today, to make these goals a reality?

- Imagine your family and personal life was perfect. What would it look like? What should you start doing more of, or less of, starting today?

- Plan your perfect calendar. Design your year from January to December as if you had no limitations. What would you change, starting today?

- Imagine that your levels of health and fitness were perfect in every way. What could you do, starting today, to make your vision for yourself into a reality?

CHAPTER 3
Clarify Your Values

One of the most important characteristics of leaders, and top people in every area of life, is that they know who they are, what they believe in and what they stand for. Average people are usually confused about their goals, values and ideals, and as a result, they go back and forth and accomplish very little. Men and women who become leaders, on the other hand, with the same or even fewer abilities and opportunities, go on to accomplish great things in whatever they attempt.

Life is lived from the inside out. The very core of your personality is your values. Your values are what make you the person you are.

Everything you do on the outside is dictated and determined by your values on the inside, whether clear or fuzzy. The greater clarity you have regarding your values on the inside, the more precise and effective will be your actions on the outside.

The Five Levels Of Personality

You can imagine your personality by thinking of a target with concentric rings, from the inside to the outside. Your personality is also made up of five rings, starting from the center, your values, and radiating outward to the next circle, your beliefs.

Your values determine your beliefs, about yourself and the world around you. If you have positive values, such as love, compassion and generosity, you will believe that people in your world are deserving of these values, and you will treat them accordingly.

Expect The Best

Your beliefs in turn determine the third ring of your personality, your expectations. If you have positive values, you will believe yourself to be a good person. If you believe yourself to be a good person, you will expect good things to happen to you. If you expect good things to happen to you, you will be positive, cheerful and future oriented.

You will look for the good in other people and situations.

The fourth level of your personality, determined by your expectations, is your attitude. Your attitude will be an outward manifestation or reflection of your values, beliefs and expectations. For example, if your value is that this is a good world to live in, and your belief is that you are going to be very successful in life, you will expect that everything that happens to you is helping you in some way. As a result, you will have a positive mental attitude toward other people and they will respond positively toward you. You will be a more cheerful and optimistic person. You will be someone that others want to work with and for, buy from, sell to and generally help to be more successful. This is why a positive mental attitude seems to go hand in hand with great success in every walk of life.

The fifth ring, or level of life, is your actions. Your actions on the outside will ultimately be a reflection of your innermost values, beliefs and expectations on the inside. This is why what you achieve in life and work will be determined more by what is going on inside of you than by any other factor.

As Within, So Without

You can always tell how a person thinks, most of the time, by looking at the conditions of their outer lives. A positive, optimistic, goal and future oriented person — on the inside — will enjoy a happy, successful and prosperous life on the outside, most of the time.

Aristotle said that the ultimate aim or purpose of human life is to achieve your own happiness. You are the very happiest when what you are doing on the outside is congruent with your values on the inside. When you are living in complete alignment with what you consider to be good and right and true, you will automatically feel happy and positive about yourself and your world.

Your goals must be congruent with your values, and your values must be congruent with your goals. This is why clarifying your values is often the starting point to high achievement and peak performance. Values clarification requires that you think through what is really important to you in life. You then organize your entire life around these values.

Any attempt to live on the outside in a manner that contradicts the values you hold on the inside will cause you stress, negativity, unhappiness, pessimism and even anger and frustration. Your chief responsibility to yourself in the creation of a great life is therefore, for you to develop absolute clarity about your values in everything you do.

Know What You Really Want

Stephen Covey once said, "Be sure that, as you scramble up the ladder of success, it is leaning against the right building." Carly Simon once sang a famous line, "Is this all there is?" Many people work hard on the outside to achieve goals that they think they want, only to find, at the end of the day, that they get no joy or satisfaction from their accomplishments. This occurs when the outer accomplishment is not in harmony with your inner values. Don't let this happen to you.

Socrates said, "The unexamined life is not worth living." This applies to your values as much as to any other area of your life. Values clarification is something you do on a "go-forward" basis. You continually stop the clock, like a time out in a football game, and ask, "What are my values in this area?"

In the Bible it says, "What does it benefit a man if he achieves the whole world but loses his own soul?" The happiest people in the world today are those who are living in harmony with their innermost convictions and values. The unhappiest people are those who are attempting to live incongruent with what they truly value and believe.

Trust Your Intuition

Self-trust is the foundation of greatness. Self-trust comes from listening to your intuition, to your "still, small voice" within. Men and women begin to become great when they begin to listen to their inner voices, and absolutely trust that they are being guided by a higher power, each step of the way.

Living in alignment with your true values is the royal road to self-confidence, self-respect and personal pride. In fact, almost every human problem can be resolved by returning to values. Whenever you experience stress of any kind, look into yourself and ask, "In what way am I compromising my innermost values in this situation?"

Watch Your Behavior

How can you tell what your values really are? The answer is simple. You always demonstrate your true values in your actions, and especially your actions under pressure. Whenever you are forced to choose between one behavior and another, you will always act consistent with what is most important and valuable to you at that moment.

Values, in fact, are organized in a hierarchy. You have a series of values, some of them very intense and important, and some of them weaker and less important. One of the most important exercises you can engage in, to determine who you really are, and what you really want, is to organize your values by priority. Once you are clear about the relative importance of your values, you can then organize your outer life so that it is in alignment with them.

Examine Your Past Behavior

There are some insightful ways to help you to determine your true values. First of all, you can look at your past. How have you behaved under pressure in the past? What choices did you make with your time or money when you were forced to choose? Your answers will give you an indication of your predominant values at that time.

Dale Carnegie once wrote, "Tell me what gives a person his greatest feeling of importance, and I will tell you his entire philosophy of life." What makes you feel important? What raises your self-esteem? What increases your sense of self-respect and personal pride? What have you accomplished in your past life that has given you the greatest sense of pride and satisfaction? These answers will give you good indications of your true values.

Determine Your Heart's Desire

The spiritual teacher Emmet Fox wrote about the importance of discovering your "Heart's Desire."

What is your heart's desire? What is it that, deep down in your heart, more than anything else, you would like to be, have or do in life? As a friend of mine asks, "What do you want to be famous for?"

What words would you like people to use to describe you when you are not there? What would you like people to say about you when you have passed on? What would you like someone to say about you at your funeral? How do you want your family, friends and children to remember you? How would you want them to talk about you after you had left this earth? How would you like people to talk to them about you?

What kind of a reputation do you have today? What kind of a reputation would you like to have sometime in the future? What would you have to begin doing today in order to create the kind of reputation that you desire?

Your Past Is Not Your Future

Many people have had difficult experiences growing up. They have fallen onto hard times and become associated with the wrong people.

They have behaved in ways that were illegal or socially unacceptable. Sometimes they have even been convicted and sent to prison for their crimes. But at a certain point in life, they decided to change. They thought seriously about the kind of person that they wanted to be known as, and thought of, in the future. They decided to change their lives by changing the values that they lived by. By making these decisions and sticking to them, they changed their lives. And what others have done, you can do as well.

Remember, "It doesn't matter where you're coming from; all that really matters is where you're going."

If you were an outstanding person, in every respect, how would you behave toward others? What sort of impression would you leave on others after you had met them and spoken with them? Imagine you could be a completely excellent person, how would you be different from today?

How Much You Like Yourself

In psychology, your level of self-esteem determines your level of happiness. Self-esteem is defined as:

"How much you like yourself." Your self-esteem, in turn, is determined by your self-image. This is the way you see yourself and think about yourself in your day-to-day interactions with others. Your self-image is shaped by your self- ideal. Your self-ideal is made up of the virtues, values, goals, hopes, dreams and aspirations that you have for yourself sometime in the future.

Here is what psychologists have discovered: The more your behavior in the moment is consistent with what you feel your ideal behavior should be, the more you like and respect yourself, and the happier you are.

On the other hand, whenever you behave in a way that is inconsistent with your ideal of your very best behavior, you experience a negative self-image. You feel yourself to be performing below your best, below what you truly aspire to. As a result, your self-esteem and your level of happiness decrease.

Perform At Your Best

The moment that you begin walking, talking and behaving in ways that are consistent with your highest ideals, your self-image improves, your self-esteem increases and you feel happier about yourself and your world.

For example, whenever you are complimented or praised by another person, or given a prize or an award for accomplishment, your self-esteem goes up, sometimes dramatically. You feel happy about yourself. You feel that your whole life is in harmony, and that you are living congruent with your highest ideals. You feel successful and valuable.

Your aim should be to deliberately and systematically create the circumstances that raise your self-esteem in everything you do. You should live your life as if you were already the outstanding person that you intend to be sometime in the future.

Know What You Believe

What are your values today with regard to your work and your career? Do you believe in the values of integrity, hard work, dependability, creativity, cooperation, initiative, ambition, and getting along well with people? People who live these values in their work are vastly more successful and more highly esteemed than people who do not.

What are your values with regard to your family? Do you believe in the importance of unconditional love, continuous encouragement and reinforcement, patience, forgiveness, generosity, warmth and attentiveness? People who practice these values consistently with the important people in their lives are much happier than people who do not.

What are your values with regard to money and financial success? Do you believe in the importance of honesty, industry, thrift, frugality, education, excellent performance, quality and persistence? People who practice these values are far more successful in their financial lives than those who do not, and far faster as well.

What about your health? Do you belicve in the importance of self-discipline, self-mastery, and self-control, with regard to diet, exercise and rest? Do you set high standards for your levels of health and fitness and then work every day to live up to those standards? People who practice these values live longer, healthier lives than people who do not.

Think Only About What You Want

Remember, you become what you think about - most of the time. Successful, happy people think about their values, and how they can live and practice those values in every part of their lives, every single day.

The big payoff is that, the more you live your life consistent with your values, the happier, healthier, more positive and energetic you will be.

Be True To Yourself

Perhaps the most important value of all is that of integrity. A billionaire once said to me, "Integrity is not so much a value in itself; it is rather the value that guarantees all the other values."

Wow! This was a great insight for me. Once you have decided that you are going to live consistent with a value, your level of integrity determines whether or not you follow through on your commitment. The more you discipline yourself to live consistent with the very best you know, the greater is your level of personal integrity. And the higher your level of integrity, the happier and more powerful you will feel in everything you do.

Truly great men and women are always described as having high levels of integrity. They live their lives consistent with their highest values, even when no one is looking. Mediocre men and women on the other hand, are always cutting corners and compromising their integrity, especially when no one is watching.

Live In Truth With Yourself and Others

Decide today to be a man or woman of honor. Resolve to tell the truth, and to live in truth with yourself and others. Crystallize your values in each area of your life. Write them down. Think of how you would behave if you were living consistent with those values, and then, refuse to compromise them for any reason.

Once you accept complete responsibility for your life, and for everything that happens to you, and then create an ideal picture of your perfect future and clarify your values, you are now ready to begin setting clear, specific goals in every area of your life. You are now on the launching ramp and ready to take off toward the stars.

Clarify Your Values:

- Make a list of your 3-5 most important values in life today. What do you really believe in, and stand for?

- What qualities and values are you best known for today among the people who know you?

- What do you consider to be the most important values guiding your relationships with others in your life?

- What are your values regarding money and financial success? Are you practicing these values daily?

- Describe your picture of an ideal person, the person you would most want to be, if you had no limitations?

- What one change could you make in your behavior today that would help you to live in greater harmony with your values?

CHAPTER 4
Determine Your True Goals

My favorite word in goal setting, and in success in general, is the word "Clarity." There is a direct relationship between the level of clarity you have about who you are and what you want, and virtually everything you accomplish in life.

Superior men and women invest the time necessary to develop absolute clarity about themselves and what they really want, like designing a detailed blueprint for a building, before they begin construction. Average people just throw themselves at life, like a dog chasing a passing car, and wonder why they never seem to catch anything, or keep anything worthwhile.

Henry David Thoreau once wrote, "Have you built your castles in the air? Good. That is where they should be built. Now, go to work and build foundations under them."

In this chapter, you begin to crystallize your visions and values into concrete goals and objectives that you can work on, every single day.

Make Your Goals Personal

Earlier I mentioned that intense, burning desire is absolutely essential to the overcoming of obstacles and the achieving of great goals. For your desire to be intense enough, your goals must be purely personal. They must be goals that you choose for yourself, rather than goals that someone else wants for you, or that you want to achieve to please someone in your life. In goal setting, for the process to be effective, you must be perfectly selfish about what is that you really, really want for yourself.

This doesn't mean that you cannot do things for other people, either at home or at work. This simply means that, in setting goals for your life, you start with yourself, and work forward.

The Great Question

One of the most important questions in goal setting is this: "What do I really want to do with my life?" If you could do or be or have anything at all in life, what would it be? Remember, you can't hit a target you can't see. You should return to this question, over and over again, in the months and years ahead. "What do I really want to do with my life?"

In determining your true goals, you start with your vision, your values and your ideals. When you begin, these will often feel a bit like fantasies, detached from reality. However, now your job is to make them concrete, like designing a dream house on paper.

Decide What You Really Want

You start with your general goals and then move to more to more specific goals:

- What are your three most important goals in your business and career, right now?

- What are your three most important financial goals right now?

- What are your three most important family or relationship goals, right now?

- What are your three most important health and fitness goals, right now?

Identify Your Major Worries

The flipside of the above questions is for you to ask, "What are my three biggest worries or concerns in life, right now?" What bothers you, worries you, concerns you, and preoccupies you, in your day-to-day life? What aggravates or irritates you? What is robbing you of happiness, more than anything else? As a friend of mine often asks, "Where does it hurt?"

Once you have identified your biggest problems, worries or concerns, ask yourself:

- What are the ideal solutions to each of these problems?

- How could I eliminate these problems or worries immediately?

- What is the fastest and most direct way to solve this problem?"

A Great Thinking Tool

In 1142, William of Ockham, a British philosopher, proposed a method of problem solving that has come to be referred to as "Ockham's

Razor." This way of thinking has become famous and popular throughout the ages. What Ockham said was that, "The simplest and most direct solution, requiring the fewest number of steps, is usually the correct solution to any problem."

Many people make the mistake of over-complicating goals and problems. But the more complicated the solution, the less likely it is ever to be implemented, and the longer the time it will take to get any results. Your aim should be to simplify the solution and go directly to the goal, as quickly as possible.

Double Your Income

For example, many people tell me that they would like to double their incomes. If they are in sales, I ask them, "What is the fastest and most direct way to double your income?" After they have come up with a series of suggestions, I give them what I consider to be the best answer. "Double the amount of time that you spend face to face with qualified prospects."

The most direct way to increase your sales has always been the same. "Spend more time with better prospects." If you don't upgrade your skills or change anything else about what you are doing, but you double the number of minutes that you spend face to face with prospects each day, you will probably double your sales income.

According to studies that go back as far as 1928, the average salesperson today spends 90 minutes each day face to face with prospects. The highest paid salespeople spend two or three times that amount. They organize their days efficiently to assure that they spend more minutes in the presence of people who can and will buy their products or services. And the more time they spend with prospects and customers, the more skilled they become at selling. The better they get, the more they sell and the more they earn, and in less time.

Double Your Productivity

If you examined your work, you would find that 20% of what you do accounts for 80% of the value of all the things you do. In my Advanced Coaching Programs, we teach our clients to identify those 20% of activities that contribute the very most value and then do twice as many of them.

Instead of using their intelligence to juggle their time and accomplish a greater number of tasks, we teach them to do fewer tasks, but tasks of higher value. Some of our clients double their productivity, and subsequently, their income in as little as 30 days with this approach, even if they have been working for many years in the same position.

Always look for the simplest and most direct way to get from where you are to where you want to go. Look for the solution that has the fewest number of steps. And most of all, take action! Get going. Get busy. Develop a "sense of urgency." The best ideas in the world are of no value until they are implemented. As the poet said, "The saddest words of mice and men are these: it might have been."

Wave A Magic Wand

In determining your true goals, use the "Magic Wand" technique. Imagine that you have a magic wand that you can wave over a particular area of your life. When you wave this magic wand, your wishes come true!

Wave a magic wand over your business and career. If you could have any three wishes in your work, what would they be? Wave a magic wand over your financial life. If you could have any three wishes in your financial life, what would they be?

Wave a magic wand over your family life and your relationships. If you could have any three wishes in this area, what would they be? If your family life were ideal in every respect, what would it look like?

Wave a magic wand over your health and fitness. If you could have any three wishes with regard to your body and your physical well- being, what would they be? If your health were perfect, how would it be different from today?

Wave a magic wand over your skills and abilities. If you could have any three skills or abilities, developed to a high level, what would they be? In what areas would you like to excel?

The magic wand technioque is fun on the one hand, but quite revealing on the other. Whenever you imagine that you have a magic wand, your true goals in that area emerge. You can also use this exercise for other people who are not sure about what they want or where they are going. It is amazing what comes out when you ask this question.

Make Up Your Dream List

In setting your true goals as an extension of imagining that you have no limitations, make up a "Dream List." A dream list is a list of everything you would like to be, have or do in your life, sometime in the future, if you had no limitations at all.

Mark Victor Hansen, co-author of Chicken Soup For the Soul, recommends that you sit down with a pad of paper and make a list of at least 100 goals that you want to accomplish in your lifetime. Then imagine that you have all the time, all the money, all the friends, all the abilities and all the resources necessary to achieve these goals. Let yourself dream and fantasize. Just write down everything that you would like to have as if you had no limitations at all.

The amazing discovery you will make is that, within 30 days after writing out this list of 100 "Dreams," remarkable things will begin to happen in your life, and your goals will start to be achieved, at a rate that you cannot even imagine today.

This seems to happen to virtually everyone once they have written down at least 100 goals. You should give it a try. You could be amazed at the results.

The Instant Millionaire

Here is another goal setting question; "If you won a million dollars tomorrow, cash, tax free, how would you change your life?"

What would you do differently? What would you get into or out of? What would you do more of or less of? What would be the first thing you would do if you learned today that you had just received one million dollars cash?

This is a way of asking the question, "How would you change your life if you were completely free to choose? The primary reason that we stay in situations that are not the best for us is because we fear change. But when you imagine that you have all the money that you will ever need, to do or be whatever you want, your true goals often emerge.

For example, if you were currently in the wrong job for you, the idea of winning a large amount of money would cause you to think about quitting that job immediately. If you were in the right job for you however, winning a lot of money would not affect your career choice at all. So ask yourself, "What would I do if I won a million dollars cash, tax free, tomorrow?"

No Fear Of Failure

Here is another question to help you clarify your true goals: What have you always wanted to do but been afraid to attempt? When you look around your world, and you look at other people who are doing things that you admire, what have you always wanted to do as well, but you have been afraid of taking the chance?

Have you wanted to start your own business? Have you wanted to run for public office? Have you wanted to embark on a new career? What have you always wanted to do but been afraid to attempt?

Do What You Love To Do

In setting goals for your life, short and long-term, you should continually ask yourself, "What do I most enjoy doing, in each area of my life?" For instance, if you could do just one thing all day long in your work, what would it be? If you could do any job or full time activity all the time, without pay, what would it be? What sort of work or activity gives you the greatest joy and satisfaction?

The psychologist Abraham Maslow identified what he called "peak experiences," those moments or times when the individual feels the happiest, most elated and exhilarated. One of your aims in life is to enjoy as many peak experiences as possible. You achieve this by thinking back and identifying those moments of peak experience in your past, and by then by imagining how you could repeat them in your present and future. What have been your happiest moments in life up to now? How could you have more of those moments in the future? What do you really love to do?

Make A Difference

You should have goals for social and community involvement and contribution as well. Think about what kind a difference you would like to make in your world. What organizations, causes, needs or social problems would you like to work on or in? What changes would you like to see? Who is there who is less fortunate than you that you would like to help?

If you were independently wealthy, what causes would you support? Most of all, what could you do today to begin making a difference in your world? Don't wait until some future date when everything will be ideal. Instead, start today in some way.

Set Clear Financial Goals

One of the most important areas of goal setting is your financial life. If you could earn and accumulate all the money you need, you could probably achieve most of your non-financial goals faster and easier than you can today.

If your life were ideal, how much money would you like to earn each month, each year? How much would you like to save and invest each month and year? How much would you like to be worth sometime in the future? What sort of estate would you like to accumulate by the time you retire, and when would you like that to be? Most people are hopelessly confused about their financial goals, but when you become absolutely clear about them for yourself, your ability to achieve them increases dramatically.

Clarity Makes Your Dreams Become Your Realities

When you are absolutely clear about what you want, you can then think about your goals, most of the time. And the more you think about them, the faster they will materialize in your life.

This process of asking yourself questions about your goals in each part of your life begins to clarify your thinking and make you a more focused and definite person. As Zig Ziglar says, "You move from being a wandering generality to becoming a meaningful specific."

Most of all, you reach the point where you can determine your major definite purpose in life. This is the springboard for great achievement and extraordinary accomplishment.

Your major definite purpose will be the topic of the next chapter, and how to achieve it will be the subject of the chapters to come.

Determine Your True Goals:

- Write down your three most important goals in life right now.

- What are your three most pressing problems or worries right now?

- If you won a million dollars cash, tax free, tomorrow, what changes in your life would you make immediately?

- What do you really love to do? What gives you the greatest feelings of value, importance and satisfaction?

- If you could wave a magic wand over your life and have anything you wanted, what would you wish for?

- What would you do, how would you spend your time, if you only had six months left to live?

- What would you really want to do with your life, especially if you had no limitations?

CONCLUSION
Take Action Today

You have now learned perhaps the most comprehensive strategy for setting and achieving goals that has ever been put together in one book. By practicing these rules and principles, you can accomplish more in the coming months and years than most people accomplish in a lifetime.

The most important quality you can develop for lifelong success is the habit of taking action on your plans, goals, ideas and insights. The more often you try, the sooner you will triumph. There is a direct relationship between the number of things you attempt and your accomplishments in life. Here are the steps for setting and achieving goals, and for living a wonderful life.

1. **Unlock Your Potential** – Always remember that your true potential is unlimited. Whatever you have accomplished in life up to now has only been a preparation for the amazing things you can accomplish in the future.

2. **Create Your Own Future** – Imagine that you have no limitations on what you can do, be or have in the months and years ahead. Think about and plan your future as if you had all the resources you needed to create any life that you desire.

3. **Clarify Your Values** – Your innermost values and convictions define you as a person. Take the time to think through what you really believe in and care about in each area of your life. Refuse to deviate from what you feel is right for you.

4. **Determine Your True Goals** – Decide for yourself what you really want to accomplish in every area of your life. Clarity is essential for happiness and high performance living.

There they are, the most important principles of goal setting and goal achieving ever discovered. Your regular review and practice of these principles will enable you to live an extraordinary life. Nothing can stop you now.

Good luck!

Want more?

For additional tips and tricks on accomplishing your goals and staying motivated, please visit our website http://www.thegoaldiggerz.com and subscribe to our email list. Can't wait to see you there!

www.ingramcontent.com/pod-product-compliance
Lightning Source LLC
Chambersburg PA
CBHW070250190526
45169CB00001B/357